The BUK Book

CW00494289

THE BUK BOOK

Musings on Charles Bukowski

by

JIM CHRISTY

Photos by

CLAUDE POWELL

ECW PRESS

Copyright © ECW PRESS, 1997

All rights reserved. No part of this publication may be reproduced, stored in a retrieval system, or transmitted in any form by any process – electronic, mechanical, photocopying, recording, or otherwise – without the prior written permission of ECW PRESS.

CANADIAN CATALOGUING IN PUBLICATION DATA

Christy, Jim, 1945–
The Buk book : musings on Charles Bukowski

ISBN 1-55022-295-3

1. Bukowski, Charles 2. Poets, American – 20th century – Biography I. Title.

PS3552.U4Z53 1997 811′.54 C96-932467-7

Design by David Johnson and Glenna Vinokur of Vinson Enterprises, Montreal.

Printed by Kromar Printing Ltd., Winnipeg, Manitoba.

Distributed in Canada by General Distribution Services, 30 Lesmill Road, Don Mills, Ontario M3B 2T6.

Distributed in the United States by Login Publishers Consortium, 1436 West Randolph Street, Chicago, Illinois, U.S.A. 60607.

Distributed in the United Kingdom by Turnaround Publisher Services, Unit 3, Olympia Trading Estate, Coburg Road, London, England N22 6TZ.

Published by ECW PRESS,
2120 Queen Street East, Suite 200,
Toronto, Ontario M4E 1E2.

http://www.ecw.ca/press

PRINTED AND BOUND
IN CANADA

"I resent life"
— Charles Bukowski

Bukowski '71
Hollywood

Claude Powell

"FOR BUKOWSKI TITLES INQUIRE AT FRONT COUNTER"

It's a sign in the poetry and fiction sections at my favorite bookstore. The manager informs me that because Charles Bukowski is, even after death, the most popular writer of literature from any country, it's best not to keep him out in the open. People steal his books. That sort of thing, however, is easier to do at the public library, despite bar codes and sophisticated security, because bookstore owners pay more attention to browsers near Bukowski. "You want to lift a book," the owner advises, "you'll have much better luck with Updike, say, or Cheever. People don't have to have them; they have to have Bukowski."

The head of the literature section at the public library reaffirms Bukowski's popularity. Despite the fact that they have to keep all his works in the closed stacks, Bukowski is still the most requested and circulated author. In fact, the librarian declares, "He is twice as popular as number two. Actually, that's a tie between Burroughs and Kerouac, and they're way ahead of whoever is third."

My examples are from Vancouver, British Columbia, Canada, and the author, although born in Germany, was intensely American. He is wildly popular in France and very big in Britain. At the time of his death, Bukowski had for several years been receiving annual royalties from Germany approaching one million dollars. I was once in a bar in Perth, Australia, and met a guy who wanted to talk about Charles Bukowski. When he found out I'd actually corresponded with the great man, I was not permitted to buy a drink – for a week.

The man is responsible for the success of an entire publishing company. Just as George Herman Ruth built Yankee Stadium, Black Sparrow Press is the house built by Henry Charles Bukowski. But old Colonel Ruppert was purchasing an established star when he grabbed the Babe from the Bosox. John Martin took a gamble on Buk, pulling him out of his

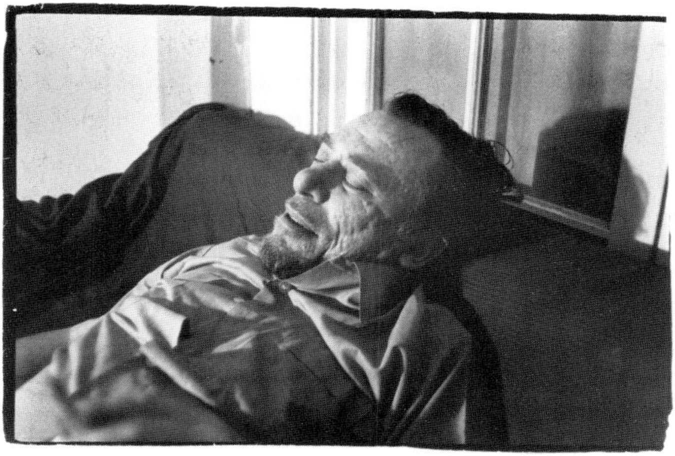

Bukowski
Hollywood '71

Claude Powell

job at the post office and the mimeograph minor leagues. And Martin has never had his Gehrig, or even much pitching to speak of. Poetry, short stories, novels – even a detective novel – and since his death, Bukowski's letters are beginning to appear. Like a guy who's gone four-for-four coming in from center field to pitch the last inning, Bukowski would write eleven poems a night and, in between novels, crank out a Hollywood screenplay.

His background bears little resemblance to that of any of his contemporaries. Some people have worked with the same material, but no one else successfully based an entire career on it. He was, and is, a phenomenon, but how do we account for this Bukowski?

He certainly didn't look like anybody's idea of a writer of literature. He was described on the fly, at the beginning of his fame, by poet Harold Norse in his autobiography *Memoirs of a Bastard Angel*: "Bukowski was misshapen – a big hunchback, with a ravaged, pockmarked face, decayed nicotine-stained teeth, and pain-filled green eyes. Flat brown hair seemed pasted to an oversized skull – hips broader than shoulders, hands grotesquely small and soft. A beer gut sagged over his belt. He wore a white shirt, baggy pants, an ill-fitting suit, the kind convicts receive when released from prison. He looked like one, down and out."

For visual emphasis of Bukowski's distinctness from other poets, one should consult Ron Mann's 1982 film *Poetry in Motion*. It is comprised of clips of American and Canadian poets reading their work and talking. Bukowski opens the movie in his weary, almost whining drawl which, by the way, Mickey Rourke gets down pretty well in *Barfly*. "Reading the great poets has been the dullest of things," he admits. "The reason poetry hasn't been appreciated is because it hasn't shown any guts, hasn't shown any dance, hasn't shown any moxie."

There is hardly a pinch of any of those ingredients in the film. No more than a soupçon in most poetry anywhere. "Poetry's generally very dull," Bukowski continues. "Those who say a poet's a special person are wrong. Generally he's just a dumb, fiddling asshole writing insecure lines that don't come through."

The next person up, Christopher Dewdney, seems to have been picked to underscore Bukowski's opinions. Then comes Michael McClure who's dull and pretentious. Many of the rest of them are downright embarrassing. There are exceptions, mainly Amiri Bakara and Michael Ondaatje. Some of the others attempt to tart up their insecure lines by adding a musical element. Their work seems particularly ridiculous when a real musician – Tom Waits – appears, accompanying himself on guitar while singing a ballad.

Bukowski's interspersed remarks provide the only intentional humor. The unintentional kind comes thanks to the antics of The Four Horsemen. The trouble is they're serious.

So is John Giorno, the worst of the bunch. You listen to him theorize and make such a big deal of what he does, and then, listening to him perform, you have to be astounded. It is not only drivel, it's horseshit.

The problem with most of these people, and with most poets and poetry everywhere, is that everything Bukowski said is true. The unsettling thing about the film is that the filmmaker apparently does not agree. You watch the film and realize the guy *likes* this stuff; you wonder, how *can* he?

Bukowski was born in Andernach on the Rhine River in Germany on August 16, 1920. His father, also Henry, was a GI from Los Angeles, who had met his future wife, Katherine Fett, two years earlier at a canteen run by her brother. Henry senior was discharged in 1922 and returned to California, where young Charles attended Virginia Road Grammar School a couple of blocks from home. His father drove a horse-drawn milk wagon. The future writer's entire childhood took place during the era encompassed

by the film *Chinatown*, just a few years after water was first piped to the city from the Owens River Valley. One of his first memories was of a family outing to the same orange groves where Jack Nicholson went looking for trouble. Bukowski would remember his parents bickering and fighting the entire trip. They bickered and fought all their lives.

Bukowski's father beat him and beat his mother too. The old man was always criticizing everybody – nobody was as good or as smart as he was. Only a cruel twist of fate was responsible for him being a milkman. He ranted and raved. "You have disgraced us!" was a refrain from Bukowski's childhood. His mother offered no solace but went along with the tyrant.

"At four or five you start putting it together and looking around," Bukowski wrote as a sixty-year-old man. "I had some pretty terrible parents and your parents are pretty much your world."

They only got worse when the Depression hit; his father lost his job, and his mother had to work as a domestic cleaning lady. The family had recently moved to a bigger house on Longwood Avenue, and the place had a lawn which the boy had to mow. But it was as much an arena, a physical and psychological torture ground, as it was a rectangle of grass. You see the kid like a young angry lion striding back and forth while the father with a whip stands over him, his tongue cracking with commands and insults. When Charles dared admit he was finished, the old man got down on his knees to examine the work, and if he saw a blade of grass sticking up higher than the others – just one in the whole lawn – he'd beat his son with a strap. Beat him until his buttocks bled. His mother said nothing except that it was for his own good.

Early on, Bukowski adopted the stance of the cool, disdainful outsider. He went through his adolescence with a knowing smirk.

His first notice for writing came in the fifth grade. Class members had been urged to go to see President Hoover at the L.A. Coliseum on Saturday and write about it for Monday. Bukowski's account was singled out by the teacher for praise. He hadn't been to see the president.

When he was fourteen his face began breaking out. Bukowski assumed it was acne, but it got worse and worse, spreading over his entire upper body. His face was covered by pus-filled boils, the size of marbles. In high school, he joined the ROTC because it was an alternative to gym class and he wouldn't, therefore, have to shower and expose his body. His ravaged face was humiliating enough.

Because his father was unemployed, Charles was able to get free treatments at the hospital. His boils were so big, they had to be drilled while he sat under an ultraviolet light and the doctors and nurses talked about him. "Geez, it's incredible, huh?" . . . "Have you ever seen anything this bad, doctor?" . . . "Never. Imagine having to walk around like that." The free treatments ended when his father got a job as a security guard at the Los Angeles County Museum.

Bukowski was so ashamed of his face that he dropped out of school in his junior year. But he returned the next semester, having in the meantime discovered two things that made his life bearable: bars and the public library.

There had been plenty of drinkers in the Bukowski and Fett families. As a kid, Bukowski had been captivated by stories of his mother's grandfather who wandered from bar to bar with his violin, passing the hat until he had enough money to stop playing and start drinking. Sixteen years old, Charles rode the streetcar downtown to joints that were lowdown enough that no one ever commented on his face.

But there was no history of reading in either family. Charles found the little library between Washington and Adams Boulevards all by himself. He read Sinclair Lewis, Hemingway, D.H. Lawrence, Upton

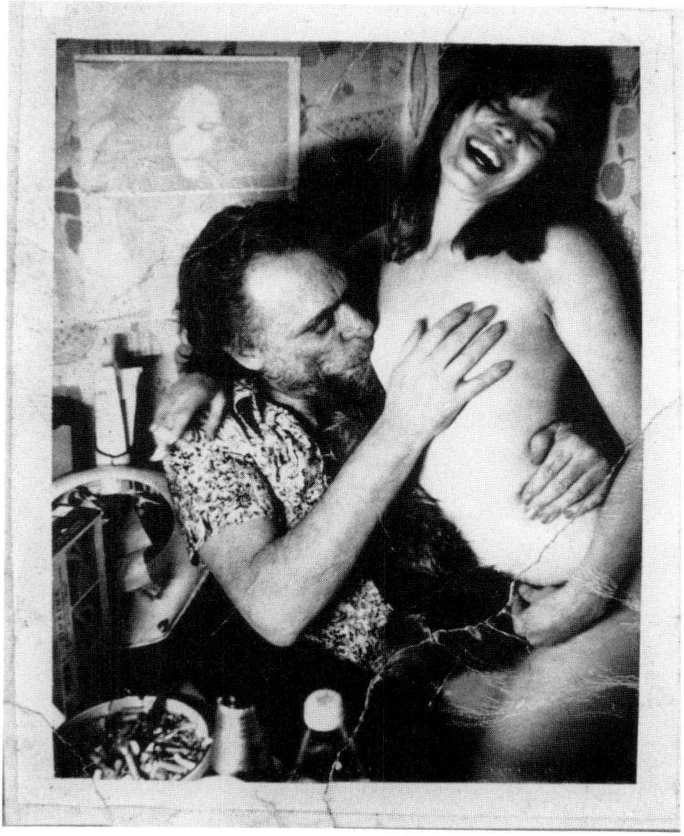

Sinclair, Carson McCullers, Knut Hamsun, and John Fante. About the same time, he began to dream of being a writer. Soon he was making his first attempts.

He graduated from high school in 1939. Prom night, no date, he went to the gym and looked in the windows at the happy couples until being chased away by a night watchman. Imagine him standing there in the dark, the introverted, acne-riddled loner. Later, he wrote that he'd known that night that his time would come. But did he really? Could he have been so confident?

He got his first job that summer, a stock boy at Sears-Roebuck on Olympic Boulevard. In the fall, he started at City College and pretended to go along with the young Nazi sympathizers only because he detested the liberals. And always would. Even more surprisingly, given his later life and literary career, he took a creative writing course.

He left home when his father went through his closet and found his writings. The old man threw them out the window, along with his clothes. Bukowski took a room on Skid Row and began his street education. Later, he recalled finding "no romantic bums."

During the winter of 1941–42, Bukowski worked at the Southern Pacific yards, cleaning railcars. In his free time, he wrote stories and drank. Bukowski had a high draft number. Having saved some money, he quit his job, bought a bus ticket to New Orleans, and began his lost years.

He left L.A. sipping whisky at the back of the bus. He had a cardboard suitcase and no illusions – no delusions either. Bukowski wasn't figuring on making his fortune; he wasn't after adventure either. He was not sallying forth in the world propelled by wanderlust. Bukowski was too cool for that. Leaving was just something to do.

How different his leaving home was from that of other writers, both his contemporaries and the people he read in libraries. That same year, Jack Kerouac, two years Bukowski's junior but far ahead of him in experience of the world, was shipping out with the merchant marine on the dangerous Murmansk run, excited about everything that was happening, taking notes on his shipmates, envisioning himself young Herman Melville. Years later, Kerouac would head across America in the other direction, movie camera eyes taking in everything, phenomenal memory storing everything, on the lookout for people who never said a commonplace thing but burned like Roman candles.

Bukowski didn't care about the corn in fields in Iowa, and everything anyone said was commonplace as far as he was concerned.

Fifteen years earlier, Thomas Wolfe had left North Carolina on the train, staying up all night, the beating of his heart echoed by the rhythm of the steel wheels, the lonesome whistle striking a chord in his soul.

Bukowski wasn't about to lose any sleep over the droning of the bus engine. He knew that nothing was waiting for him at the next stop except another dumb job and lousy room. Bukowski hated Thomas Wolfe.

Henry Miller heading west to get over a woman; William Saroyan heading east to take the world by storm. Charles Bukowski would take an easy job, and as for women, he'd never had one to get over. In New Orleans, he got his cheap room and a job in an auto parts warehouse. After a few weeks, he started back for the coast, working his passage on a railroad track crew. During a stopover in El Paso, Bukowski discovered Dostoevski's *Notes from Underground.* From Los Angeles, he went to San Francisco, where he lived for a few weeks selling blood to the Red Cross. He crossed the country again on a bus and was arrested in Philadelphia for draft evasion. He did a couple of months in Moyamensing Prison before a psychiatrist gave him a 4F status. He was working at another parts place in Philadelphia when he lost his virginity to a fat woman he met in a bar. He was twenty-four years old.

He was in St. Louis a couple of months later when his first story, "Aftermath of a Lengthy Rejection Slip," was published in *Story Magazine*. It had been done from frustration, from experience. Everything else he'd written, and he'd been writing all the time, was made up, literary, contrived. The story may not have been much but it was real.

Philadelphia had good connotations for Bukowski, so he returned there after the war, staying until the middle of 1946. Here he had the fights, with a bartender named Thomas McGilligan, that would find their way – forty years later and transplanted to an alley in Los Angeles – into the movie *Barfly*.

Back in Los Angeles, Bukowski met Jane Cooney Baker, the woman portrayed by Faye Dunaway in *Barfly*. They started drinking together one afternoon in a bar at Glenview and Alvarado, and kept drinking until she died ten years later.

It was a tumultuous affair, on again, off again. At times they made an attempt at something approaching normal housekeeping. It was the first time in his life Bukowski had decent and regular sex. Before, there were only whores and drunken bar pickups. In 1952, he took a temporary job at the post office, and it lasted three years.

One day he felt sick at work, went home, and

collapsed. He was taken to the charity ward of the same hospital where he used to go to have his boils lanced. The ambulance stacked patients in tiers; Bukowski was on the top tier, bleeding from mouth and rectum, bleeding on the people below.

Upon his release, Bukowski was told he was lucky to have survived a bleeding ulcer. He was warned never to drink again. He went directly to a bar and had a beer.

He resigned from the post office, and Jane Cooney Baker introduced a new meaning to his life: she took him to the racetrack and explained how things worked.

Not long after this introduction, Jane threw him out.

Bukowski had recently begun to write poetry for the first time. He was thirty-five years old. He bought a magazine that listed poetry outlets and sent some poems to a journal in Texas called *Harlequin*. The editor, Barbara Frye, accepted his poems, writing him that he was a genius. They corresponded and Frye declared that no man would ever marry her. Bukowski wrote back, "I'll marry you."

She came to Los Angeles and Bukowski met her bus, not knowing what to expect. She'd never sent a picture. Frye turned out to be a good-looking, young blond. They went to Las Vegas and got married. That night, Bukowski made two startling discoveries. The first was that she was sexually insatiable; the second was that she was worth millions of dollars.

They went to her hometown of Wheeler, Texas. Both of them could have lived to be two hundred years old without ever having to work, but Barbara insisted on having a job to show her independence. When Bukowski wasn't stocking shelves in a drug-store, he walked the dusty streets of Wheeler smoking cigars and being laughed at by the locals.

After three months, they went to L.A. and Barbara got a job in the sheriff's department. They both edited *Harlequin* and went to art classes at L.A. City College.

One morning, seven a.m., there was a knock on the door. Bukowski got out of bed. The man at the door served him with divorce papers. He went back to bed, and after making love with Barbara, he left. She let him keep the car.

He wrote a short story called "How I Threw Away a Million Dollars."

It was in the work done after his divorce that the Bukowski image, the actual Bukowski, sometimes called Chinaski, began to make an appearance. The literary trappings were cast off; the literary trick was in being himself. He had been a bum, a lumpen proletarian, a drunk; well, so be it. Of course, others

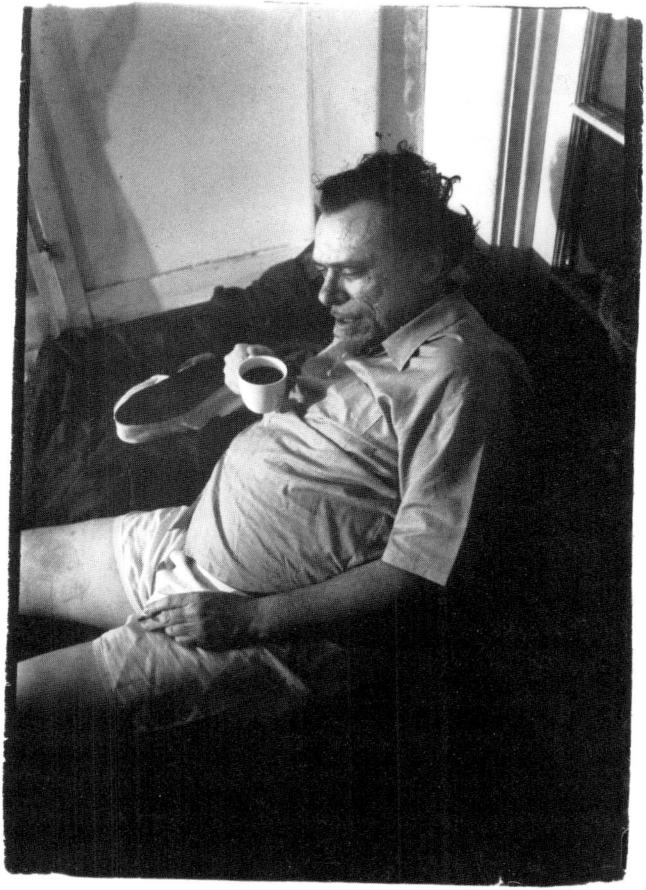

Bukowski '71
Hollywood

Claude Powell

had worked the same territory, but what would eventually set Bukowski apart from the rest of them – the Knut Hamsuns, Jack Londons, Maxim Gorkys, and Jim Tullys – was that Bukowski was funny. Sometimes the humor was black, sometimes it was near slapstick, but he was nearly always funny.

Bukowski's mother died in 1957; his father, the next year. The old man left him a house in Temple City, east of L.A., near Santa Anita Racetrack. Bukowski sold the place for $16,000. He made out as if he went through the money quickly, and much of it did go to Santa Anita, but a lot of it went into the bank. Not long after his father died, Bukowski returned to the post office. He'd be there twelve years, until 1970, sitting hunched over on that stool, hour after hour, day after day, year after year. His real life was lived at home, wherever that happened to be, hunched over a typewriter, beer, wine at hand, radio on, turned to a station that played classical music. Poems spilled out of what Bukowski called "the typer." He began to have some small success. His first book, a chapbook of fourteen pages called *Flower, Fist and Bestial Wail*, appeared in 1960, an offset print job from something called Hearse Press. Other small books appeared soon afterwards: *Poems and Drawings* from Epos in 1962; *Longshot Poems for Broke Players*, 7 Poets Press,

1962; *Run with the Hunted*, Midwest Press, 1962. The last outfit was run by a guy named R.R. Cuscaden, an insurance underwriter and trade magazine editor who was interested in alternatives not only to the typical "tea cosy" poetry but to beat writing as well. Cuscaden was the first person to ever write about Bukowski, an essay in the spring–summer 1962 issue of a review called *Satis*: "Charles Bukowski: Poet in a Ruined Landscape." Soon other essays by other people began to appear in the small magazines.

Most Bukowski admirers, both in the early days and later, were people who either wished they could be like him (but never would be) or pretended to be like him (but never would be, could be, or had been). Rarely would Bukowski ever have a literary acquaintance, whether in person or epistolary, who was as tough as he was. In 1961, when he began a correspondence with Jon Edgar Webb, his first important publisher, Bukowski met his match.

Webb, twenty years older than Bukowski, owned Loujon Press and published *The Outsider*, the best literary magazine of its time. He'd grown up in Cleveland and been a police reporter on the *Plain Dealer*. Webb did a three-year stretch in Mansfield Reformatory in the thirties for armed robbery. Inside, he edited the prison paper, *The New Day*. When he got out, Webb knocked around for years and wrote tough stories about his experiences.

The first issue of *The Outsider* appeared in the fall of 1961. Webb's star was Henry Miller, but he devoted his third issue to Bukowski. Webb promoted Buk's image, and in doing so he was affirming his own stance and experience.

In the summer of 1964, Webb and his wife, Gypsy Lou, came out to visit Bukowski. Ostensibly they were to talk about book projects but mostly they drank.

Bukowski returned the visit, going back to New Orleans for the first time since 1942. He hadn't even been out of Southern California for ten years. The Webbs lived in a dank basement where they also stored their press. Bukowski stayed around the corner in a house owned by Minnie Seagate, who operated a restaurant called the Cajun Kitchen. She fed him and did his laundry. The Webbs wouldn't let him in their place unless he showed up with new poems. Some days he brought fifteen of them. The result of this visit was Bukowski's first real book, *Crucifix in a Deathhand*, in 1965.

While this book was in the works, Bukowski had been corresponding with a woman named Frances Smith. A friend had shown her one of Bukowski's poems and she'd written to him. Eventually she sent

Bukowski '71
Hollywood

Claude Powell

him her phone number, and they began spending time together. When Frances was much younger, she'd published some poems, but marriage and raising four kids had put an end to that sort of thing. Bukowski encouraged her to start writing again. When she got pregnant, they moved in together, and their daughter, Marina Louise, was born on September 7, 1964.

Picture the domestic scene: Bukowski, Frances, and an infant daughter living in a small apartment. He comes home from the post office, his back aching from sorting mail, his neck aching; he has a headache. The sink is piled with dirty dishes, a pail holds dirty diapers. Frances has been cooped up at home all day. He starts writing and drinking, the phone starts ringing, visitors show up, many of them would-be poets who want to impress the tough guy with how much they can drink. Frances is fed up with all of it and an argument ensues. It wasn't meant to last.

Bukowski moved out, moved his routine to another cheap apartment. He was becoming more and more well known. More books appeared from obscure outfits. Publishers of offset or mimeograph magazines from across the country solicited his work. One of these was Doug Blazek, who edited *Ole* from his home in Bensenville, Illinois. What distinguished Blazek from the rest of the small-press crowd, besides the fact that he became a good poet himself, was that he got Bukowski writing prose again, something he'd given up when he'd gone into the hospital with a bleeding ulcer. Realizing Bukowski's popularity, Blazek published several of his short prose pieces as chapbooks. *Confessions of a Man Insane Enough to Live with Beasts* appeared in 1965; *All the Assholes in the World and Mine*, the next year. Much of the writing is gauche and sophomoric. But young writers are entitled to be gauche and sophomoric, and Bukowski, in his mid-forties, was a young writer. Only people like John Updike and William Dickey have never been jejune.

They had begun to publish him in Europe, and in 1966 Bukowski started corresponding with Carl Weissner in Germany. Weissner was born during the war in Karlsruhe and grew up with U.S. soldiers in his neighborhood. Many of the GIs were black, and Weissner picked up on their slang and on jazz. He started reading Henry Miller and Jack Kerouac. He brought out a magazine called *Klacktoveedsedsteen*, after a Charlie Parker tune. Bukowski replaced Kerouac as Weissner's literary hero. Bukowski replaced Kerouac as many people's literary hero. Eventually, as his German translator, Weissner would be worth millions to Bukowski.

In the late sixties, Bukowski was like a miner who'd been trapped underground for decades, with just enough oxygen to breathe, licking the walls for moisture; now the first of the rescue crew had shown up, and Bukowski's response was typical of one so long deprived: he was by turns sweetly thankful and downright obnoxious.

"Ninety-nine percent of the worst human beings I've ever met," remarked Kenneth Rexroth, no Saint Francis himself, "are poets." Well, is it any wonder? You sit alone agonizing over an obscure arrangement of words on a page that few people in the world have any interest in whatsoever and most of those are other poets or people who want to be poets, and if they read what you've written it's only to seek evidence that they are better than you are. If you're lucky, they'll get the evidence, but woe unto you should they not, for if they admit, deep down in their heart of hearts, that your talent in this hole-in-corner world exceeds their own, they will make your life hell in whatever way possible, whether by vicious review or malicious gossip.

Who are these people anyway? Frustrated, diddling, insecure creeps, for the most part, but with a few genuine heroes tossed in. The usual male poet is a guy who threw like a girl, and the usual female poet, a nerd's femme fatale. In high school, they could only

get dates with each other. Nowadays they all go to university and take creative writing courses, graduate and teach creative writing.

Every so often a poet would come along who didn't fit that background. He or she, with rare exception, didn't last. In the 1950s, a bunch of exceptions appeared all at once and a generation was created around them. These were Charles Bukowski's contemporaries. The notion of Beatnik Buk is absurd.

In 1967 Bukowski began contributing a weekly column, "Notes of a Dirty Old Man," to an "underground" paper in Los Angeles, *Open City*, which had a circulation of several thousand. That summer, heady with success, he visited Jon and Gypsy Lou Webb in Tucson, Arizona, where they had relocated for health reasons. Bukowski seemed deliberately contrary once he saw the latest work from Loujon Press, Henry Miller's *Order and Chaos chez Hans Reichel*. Bukowski's pettiness might have been excused as a temporary fit of jealousy had the Webbs published the work of some new and inferior discovery, but Miller had cleared the ground upon which Bukowski was taking his first toddler's steps. He had already begun to call himself America's greatest writer – "number one, baby" – and maybe new evidence that the guy who wrote *Tropic of Cancer* and

Tropic of Capricorn was still around made him feel insecure. It brought out his arrogance when he should have been humble.

Harold Norse wrote that there were two Bukowskis, and five o'clock separated them. "Before five he was a lamb, literally sheepish with shame and guilt." After five, Bukowski "had an insulting mockery in his voice; his aim was to crush others. . . . He never tired of bragging and boasting, of clamoring for attention. His competitive spirit, arrogance and macho pose were irritating. . . . I believe his eyes got their color from envy and jealousy."

One afternoon in the spring of 1966, Bukowski had come home from work and was at the machine, bottle of beer at his side, when there was a knock at his door, but this time the person on the other side was neither a poet who wanted to catch some reflected fire nor a girlfriend looking to create some sparks. It was the manager of a furniture and office supply company who was going to change Bukowski's life, who was going to take him to the big time.

His name was John Martin. He'd been impressed by a Bukowski poem in *The Outsider*. Martin wanted to be a publisher, and he wanted to start with Charles Bukowski. This was all right by Buk. That spring and summer Martin produced three broadsides of

Bukowski's poetry and paid the author thirty dollars for each. He used his company's printing press. When these items proved extremely successful, Martin was encouraged to proceed with his real dream of bringing out beautiful books. He quit his job and sold his own extensive book collection to finance Black Sparrow Press. The first work appeared in 1968, a volume of Bukowski's poetry, *At Terror Street and Agony Way*.

This was followed in 1969 by another poetry volume, *The Days Run Away Like Wild Horses Over the Hills*. It was Bukowski's bust-out year. He appeared with Norse and Philip Lamantia in a volume of the Penguin Modern Poets series, and his columns from the underground newspaper were published by Essex House. Weissner translated *Notes of a Dirty Old Man* and got it published in Germany.

Bukowski was on his way, and after twelve years, he left the post office. Much has been made, mostly by Bukowski himself, about what a courageous move this was, plunging boldly into the unknown. He wrote that he was gambling on Martin and himself, trusting that fate would allow him to exist on the small monthly allowance guaranteed by Martin. Actually, besides this money and what he'd been banking religiously for years, Bukowski had retirement benefits, and royalties. Not only were his poetry books paying off,

Dirty Old Man had sold twenty thousand copies the first year.

He quit January 1, 1970, seven months short of his fiftieth birthday. By January 21, he'd finished his first novel, *Post Office*. Martin brought it out a year later and it was an immediate success. From now on, every book Bukowski wrote was an immediate success.

He began to do readings, locally at first, but by 1972 Bukowski was flying around the country, from one raucous event to the next. They weren't so much readings as wild spectacles, unprecedented in literary history. Bukowski discovered half the audience came to worship him, the other half to heckle. Most of them were drunk, and he had to be drunk to start the reading, drunker to get through the ordeal.

Lawrence Ferlinghetti, the poet and founder of City Lights Press, had started corresponding with Bukowski in 1969, and wanted to publish anything that wasn't promised to John Martin. The first book was a prose collection called *Erections, Ejaculations, Exhibitions and General Tales of Ordinary Madness*, published in 1972. Ferlinghetti brought Bukowski to San Francisco in September 1973 for a reading at the Telegraph Hill Neighborhood Center. When Bukowski made his appearance to a packed house of screaming fans, Ferlinghetti knew he had a star.

Bukowski made the trip with Linda King, the woman he'd been going with for two years. When they met in 1970, Bukowski hadn't had sex in four years. When they weren't making up for Bukowski's lost time, they were fighting, but they didn't let either activity interfere with their drinking. At a party after the reading, in an apartment over the City Lights bookstore, Buk and Linda got into it. They broke windows and tumbled down stairs. Hank claimed Linda attacked him and scratched his face. Linda maintained she didn't scratch him, all she did was bite him. The battle made the San Francisco *Chronicle*, which reported Linda's remark, "I think I would kill him if he wasn't so good in bed."

If one of Bukowski's big-name contemporaries had gotten into a scene like that, his or her reputation would have been severely damaged. Imagine John Irving involved in that sort of thing. Bukowski's reputation was only enhanced.

There was another San Francisco reading later that year, organized by Joe Wolberg of City Lights Bookstore and held at the War Memorial Building. Like any true star, Bukowski could make demands and have them fulfilled. All he wanted was a fridge stocked with beer by his side on the stage. Poet A.D. Winans, a friend of Buk's and a post office worker himself, was there, and he recalls Bukowski "emptying one bottle after another, all the time engaging in verbal combat with a small group of feminists who had come to taunt him. . . . [T]hey lost the fight."

There were also the usual hecklers and jealous poets, many of whom demanded to get on stage and read themselves. Bukowski would have none of it. Winans recalls that at the end of the reading the crowd was yelling for more.

Winans was at the party afterwards too. "[I]t was wall-to-wall bodies . . . young poets who were jealous of the old man" and plenty of "old enemies." Everyone was trying to get next to Bukowski and impress Bukowski. One woman had a male slave on a leash. Later, Winans found these two in the washroom. She was giving him a golden shower, and told Winans he could watch. Winans declined. The next time he went to the washroom, "Buk was getting a blow job from the hostess of the party."

The readings and the yearly volumes had the effect of riots. He was an incontinent bull in the literary teashop, his reputation a mad dog from hell. In comfortable literary circles, which means most literary circles, Bukowski was their biggest nightmare, a horrible dream they never thought could come true. But away from these circles, and just about anywhere, he was just what was wanted. Young men and young

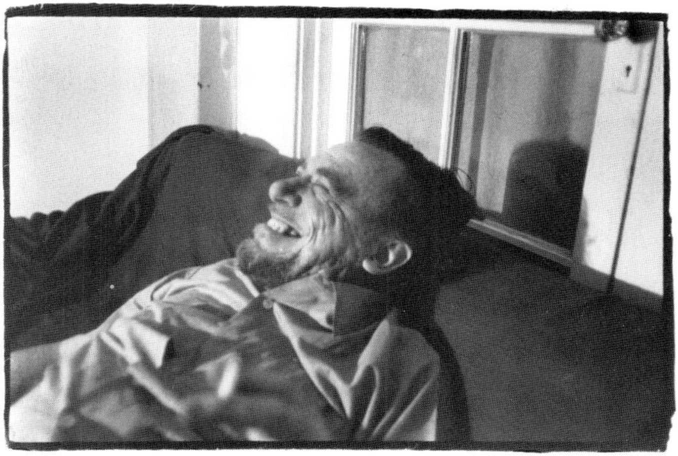

Bukowski
Hollywood '71

Claude Powell

women all over the universe wrote him letters and he wrote back. Publisher and editor Kevin Ring in Warks, England, has a vast Bukowski correspondence. Publisher and editor Trevor Reeves in Dunedin, New Zealand, has a vast Bukowski correspondence. Someday I expect to be walking along the beach near Papeete and meet somebody with a sheaf of Buk missives.

Quite a Bukowski cult developed in New Zealand, and it revolved around the activities of the appropriately named Caveman Press. Besides Bukowski, Caveman published another American, junkie poet William Wantling. At the center of all this literary excitement in the mid-seventies was Trevor Reeves, who says the goal was "primarily to break up the narrow styles and concerns, as we saw them, of resident NZ writers."

Nearly twenty-five years later, I met Reeves in Dunedin, where he is still involved in publishing. He considers Bukowski to be as important now as he ever was. "I'm in my mid-fifties, so I look at him differently than I did as a kid. But we need him now if only as an antidote to political correctness."

Reeves, who became a Christian in the eighties, sees a religious element in Bukowski's work. "Underneath everything else is a compassion and honesty, a really brave stance in the face of the trials of life."

Most writers, as Bukowski has emphasized, lead dull lives and that explains their dull writing. For the most part these dull people associate with other dull people, also writers or in the writing business. Their biographies are filled with comments from other writers. Every once in a while there appears a writer who has known regular human beings and spent considerable time with them. Biographers seem constitutionally unable to grasp this fact and, consequently, ignore important people in the odd writer's life. A dozen biographies have been written about Jack Kerouac, and all of them sum up the last ten years of his life in a few pages. It's not because this decade was without incident, it's simply that the writer removed himself from literary entanglements. The assumption must be that Kerouac's associates, not being writers or in any way connected with the cultural scene, could not possibly have anything to say about him that would be important.

An even more obvious example of this sort of thing was the first biography of crime writer Jim Thompson, a Bukowski-league drinker who didn't even know another writer. It evidently never occurred to Michael J. McCauley, author of *Jim Thompson: Sleep with the Devil*, to go where the writer went: bars. The result is a work consisting of little more than a series of plot summations and notes on where Thompson was living at the time of composition.

Bukowski was forty years old before he met any writers, and after that it was difficult to avoid them. Part of him loved the adulation, and Bukowski played up to his image, but when he wanted to escape, he went to the racetrack or hung a Do Not Disturb sign on the door of his apartment. When he had a choice in his companions, Bukowski preferred whoever happened to be around, the old man down the hall or a kid off the street.

Claude Powell was a kid off the street when he met Buk, or Hank, as he was usually called, in 1969 at the Venice Cafe in Venice, California. The cafe sponsored nightly poetry readings, and Bukowski was sort of the main event, even if he wasn't reading. The owners kept him primed with beer and wine. Powell and his party had smuggled in a bottle of rye, which appealed to Bukowski who was eager to share the bottle with them in the washroom. Powell remembers Bukowski chasing girls, "grinning quite large, a demonic nasal laugh with his nose all twisted. . . . 'Heh, heh, heh' he's saying."

After the cafe closed for the night, Bukowski invited Powell to a party at Steve Richmond's home in Ocean

Park, then a rundown area between Venice and Santa Monica. Powell remembers Richmond as "a budding poet and quite broke and his apt. looked it."

Besides writing poetry, Richmond worked in a bookstore and published a little mimeographed magazine that included Bukowski's work. Richmond had given up a career as a lawyer to live this bohemian existence.

There were forty or fifty people crammed into his apartment, all doing "pills, booze, pot and acid," in the eerie light of "huge crazy-looking lifesized black twisted upturned macabre waxed candles." Powell's premier memory of this event is of Bukowski "pulling his pants down around his ankles and calling Steve's bitch dog over to lick his balls. What a wonderful sight with Bukowski looking backwards through his legs and the dog's nose stuck up the crack of his ass. Those of us still standing loved it!"

Powell maintained the presence of mind to think, "This guy Bukowski is sure full of his own shit but ain't we all."

Bukowski was besieged by young poets, most of them pretentious sycophants. He liked Claude because, although he was the same age as many of the poets, Powell was unaffected, had an appetite for life, and couldn't care less that Bukowski was on his way to becoming a big-time writer. Buk gave Claude his address and phone number, and his new friend began to visit him on DeLongpre Street in East Hollywood at his "simple one bedroom court apartment, first one on the right if you were facing them."

Bukowski, at the time, favored wine and Hamms beer and was usually to be found at the typewriter set on the kitchen table with one drink or another or both at his side. If he wasn't typing away, Buk might be busy with his little drawings of dogs, flowers, and gnomish people with cigarettes stuck in the corners of their mouths.

But with the arrival of visitors, that drinking became serious, so much so at times that the LAPD would visit. One night they burst through the door in their blue windbreakers and ball caps, toting .12-gauge pump-action riot guns. They started hollering, pushing people around and poking them with the ends of the guns. One guy had his weapon levelled at Bukowski, who sat back on the filthy couch in his T-shirt and underwear and began bad-mouthing the men in blue. His action focused the attention of the cops. In the midst of the police threats, Bukowski interrupted to tell the head cop, "Some people think I'm IMMORTAL."

Powell reasons that Bukowski, by becoming such a handful, knocked the police so off their stride that a bust was avoided. After taking names, the LAPD departed.

Bukowski could be a sweet guy but not often, and not, as Harold Norse said, after five o'clock. One afternoon, before five o'clock, Claude was telling Bukowski about the difficulty he was having getting close to a girl he was interested in, called Kathy. He would meet her after work and they'd neck in her car, but whenever Claude asked her out, she demurred because she was living with a guy, the filmmaker Les Blank. Claude was frustrated, feeling that wasn't enough of a reason; this was the early seventies, after all. Bukowski told the kid not to worry, he'd fix things up for him, so they drove over to where Kathy and Blank lived in a quiet residential area of Hollywood, in an apartment in their landlord's house. When they showed up, "Kathy was skeptical but Les Blank was beside himself to have Hank as an uninvited guest."

Blank broke out the wine and showed them his bedroom editing room complete with rented Moviola. "He really tried to make Hank and me comfortable."

Things were all right for a couple of hours, during which time plenty of wine was consumed. The scene changed though when Bukowski began trying to kiss Kathy, who wanted nothing to do with him. Bukowski's response to her rejection was to tell Claude in a

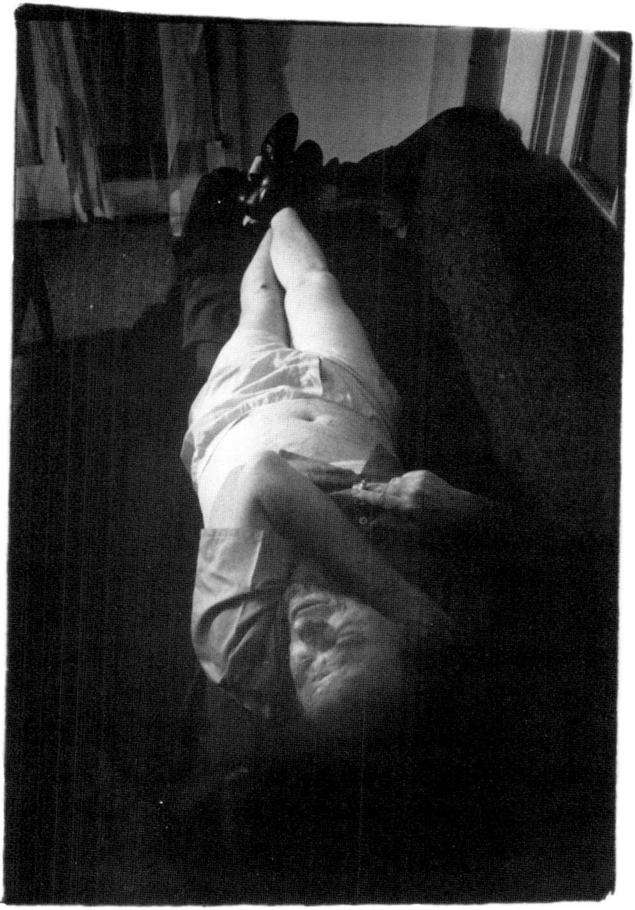

Bukowski '71
Hollywood

Claude Powell

loud voice that "she was too skinny for any man's taste and that he wouldn't want her anyway after she'd been living with FAT BOY – which is what he'd begun calling Les."

Kathy, on the verge of tears, took Claude aside and told him to get the monster out of there. But Hank had just begun. First he went over to Blank who was seated on the couch with his cat. Bukowski spit a mouthful of wine on the filmmaker and another mouthful on the cat. A moment later Bukowski was back again, "And threatened to beat Les' ass because he could smell pussy all over him."

Blank merely grinned, walked into his bedroom, and came back with a pen and a copy of Bukowski's *Notes of a Dirty Old Man*, which he asked the dirty old man to please sign. "Hank took it in his two hands, opened it and spat into the middle of it and closed it."

The next thing, everyone is in the backyard name-calling, hissing, and screaming. Hank threw a couple of punches at Les who easily avoided them, meanwhile still asking for an autograph.

Bukowski fell into the landlord's tulip beds and took swings at anyone who tried to get him out. It required Claude, Les, and the landlord to get Bukowski into the car. "Back at Hank's place, Hank wanted to know if we had straightened everything out! I assured him he had settled all that was going on between Kathy and me forever."

In 1971, Bukowski moved to another court apartment on Carlton Way just in back of Hollywood and Western. By coincidence, two friends of Claude's lived in the same court, and Claude, who'd been in Florida, showed up to find them – Rod and Gina are good aliases – sitting on chairs and a naked Charles Bukowski on their bed. "Hank had his dick in his hand and he was pulling on his chicken neck laughing at me looking down on him." The famous writer added, "And this is why you came back to L.A. Just to look at my purple dick."

Rod and Claude took a walk around the block to cut up jackpots, leaving Gina alone with Bukowski. Rod kept chanting, "I've got a Buk in my bed."

Bukowski had recently taken up with Linda King, "who was pretty hot tempered when it came to all these women and girls who were taking an interest in poetry all of a sudden." Powell suggests that part of King's jealousy could be attributed to the fact that Bukowski had become a successful poet. She believed she was just as good.

As for the women, and the theme of the novel by the same name, Powell sums both up precisely: "He had lived the life of a loner for so long and he was enjoying the sudden attention. He lived like he was holding court."

The great writer spent a couple of months with King in her home in the Silverlake area of Los Angeles. But one night as Claude sat at the dining room table drinking with Rod and Gina, there was a knock on the door. It was a forlorn Bukowski in an old pair of pants, tweed jacket, and wingtips. He'd just fled Linda King's place, getting out by the skin of his teeth but without his shirt and socks. Hank told the tale and the booze flowed. After several hours, Claude, who'd recently become interested in photography, asked Hank if he could take some pictures of him with his new Polaroid. Bukowski said, "Sure, kid." And leaned back "all proud, with a cigar in his mouth."

The results inspired Gina to remark that he looked downright pitiful in those pictures, poor man, and him just losing his girl. She set out to change his expression, beginning a slow, shot-by-shot striptease. By the time the evening ended, they had all taken turns being photographed "doing dirty things with Gina."

The next afternoon, Bukowski invited his young friends over to his apartment – which he'd had the foresight to maintain when he moved in with Linda King – to meet Joe Wolberg, who'd come down from

Bukowski
Hollywood '71

Claude Powell

City Lights in San Francisco. The next year, Wolberg would organize the first of Bukowski's riotous San Francisco readings, but his current project was a large volume of Hank's poetry.

It started out as a fine afternoon. "There's a few beers and some smoke. Hank goes to his closet a couple times and shows us he's drawing his little caricatures in color now, with crayons he stole from his daughter the last time he visited her. He's so proud."

During the course of the conversation, the polaroids from the night before get mentioned, and Wolberg says he'd like to see them. Powell shows them to him, and he's impressed, believes he could use them in the middle of the poetry book. "This is great, things are mellow, Bukowski is acting like a gentleman."

The doorbell rings but before anyone can answer, Linda King bursts in ready to rumble. Right away she sees the polaroids and hollers, "This is what I'm talking about, Hank! You bastard!"

King makes a quick two-handed grab of the polaroids and begins ripping them to pieces. Bukowski, attempting to rescue them, instead falls directly onto the coffee table, crushing the top and all four legs. Rod and Claude, trying to subdue Linda, knock Gina down and soon join her on the floor. While thrashing around, Claude caught a glimpse of Joe Wolberg, "standing in the middle of Hank's sofa wide-eyed, trapped from reaching the front door."

When Linda sees Gina on the floor, she grabs her by the hands to pull her close for some inside fighting. Unfortunately, Gina, just a few days before, had broken her little finger playing baseball. "Linda," Claude recalls, "grabbed her metal-splinted pinkie and bent it completely backwards."

The girl's screams apparently ended Linda's anger. Gina ran out of the apartment, everyone presuming she'd fled to her own place. She had, but a few minutes later, Gina returned with her .38 revolver. Linda, fortunately for her, had departed by then.

Rod and Claude took Gina to the emergency room, Joe Wolberg went back to San Francisco, and it was months before Hank did anything about the squashed coffee table. "He said he liked it that way."

But there were islands of calm. There had to be for the man to do his work. Bukowski wrote dozens of books, a fact that was overlooked by all those who wanted him to come out and play, at their convenience. Later in his life, he was harassed by people wanting him to drink all night with them, take a swing at somebody, and jump on top of their wives or girlfriends, or someone else's.

Bukowski was one of only three writers of his time who became "role models." The other two were Jack Kerouac and Hunter S. Thompson. The idea, evidently, was that their way led to wisdom, or some mystical reward. But the kind of behavior Thompson and Bukowski have inspired is mostly bad. All Kerouac's image is responsible for is generations of people going on the road and experimenting with compassion. The autobiographical writings of Thompson and Bukowski got people drinking and ingesting drugs all night, and, generally, acting rude. But the people these two inspired are of thoroughly different types. Thompson was adulated by the solidly middle class. Young people, men mostly, who ardently pursued their career goals while consciously working on their image. Knuckling under all week to their journalism school assignment or the demands of the pressroom but on Friday night buying a bottle of Wild Turkey with the Mastercard. A sort of gonzo frat house routine.

One thing about being like Bukowski: those drunk tanks were real and so were the LAPD coming through the door; likewise the beatings by the Philadelphia bartender, the grappling with the fat Philadelphia whore, the stupid jobs, and the bleeding from the rectum.

You could act like those three but writing like them – there's the rub.

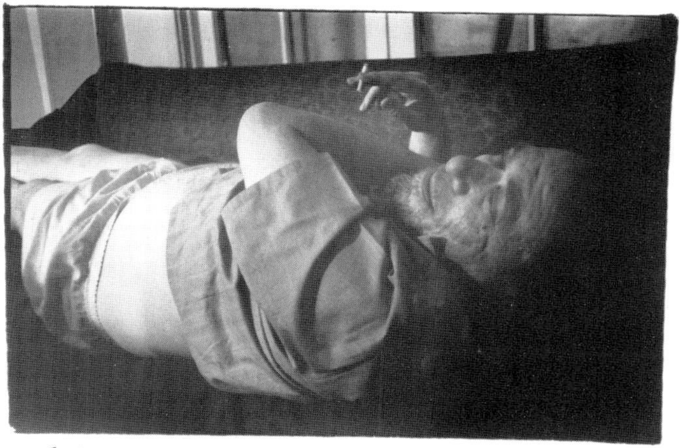

Bukowski
Hollywood '74

Claude P[illegible]

Like the other two, Bukowski worked hard. "There would be long periods when the No Visitors sign was out." Powell remembers that Bukowski's typing could be heard all through the court at Carlton Way. He typed in the kitchen on a manual Underwood on a metal-rimmed formica table.

Bukowski did not, however, work in spurts; he worked all the time, the poetry and short stories done on the fly. The time of No Visitors was the time of novel writing. "Hank called his typing, Playing the Piano." When Bukowski wasn't playing his piano, it didn't mean he wasn't working. Once, Rod and Claude became exceptionally curious about the silence, and they sneaked around the outside of his apartment, "to see if we could get a peek of Hank doing something immortal."

Once they spied on him for a day and a half. He was laying flat out on his back in bed with a pink blanket pulled up to his chin while he stared at the ceiling. He never seemed to move or close his eyes.

They were respectful of his sober work periods, but one time, after the typing had been going on seemingly for days without a pause, Rod and Claude got into position under Bukowski's window. "We hollered up for him to play 'My Heart Is a Hobo' next."

The typing stopped. They heard the chair slide

back. Bukowski's face appeared at the window and he hollered, "Go away, kids!"

Some of the best times Claude Powell spent with Bukowski, over the several years of their friendship, were at the Western Sizzler restaurant on Hollywood Boulevard. "Hank was hard but there were soft spots in the tough guy too."

These were allowed to be revealed at the Sizzler. "He knew my money wasn't too big so he'd lead me around the corner, telling me how if you're going to drink you gotta keep your strength up with meat." Away from the madness, they'd have regular conversations, Bukowski being solicitous of his young pal.

But Bukowski could only be placid for so long; it might take a day, a week, or even a month, but you could bet he'd return raging, like a wild bull bursting out of the Sizzler. And woe unto anyone Bukowski's bloodshot eyes fastened upon when he began to paw the ground. Like poor Bob Lind.

You remember him? He had a big hit song in 1966, "Elusive Butterfly." Claude Powell had met him, and one evening when things were slow, Claude got the idea of introducing Bukowski to the singer-songwriter.

"Things started off okay," Powell remembers. "Intros were made, some beer and wine came out."

But as the evening wore on, Lind "started baring his soul," complaining about how "Elusive Butterfly" had taken him to stardom but then things got tough, and to put up with it all, he'd had to resort to booze and pills for propellant.

During Lind's litany of complaints, Bukowski appeared bored, and Powell knew where that could lead. Finally, Bukowski said, "Look, Bob, your troubles are petty. What you need is a kick in the ass, get you straightened out and headed in the right direction. If one song is all you have, one song is all you have. Accept it. No one likes a whiner."

Bob blinked a couple of times and his jaw quivered. He sniffed, and cleared his throat, said he had another song. He brought out his guitar. "The rest of my future is riding on this one. I'd like to do it for you. It's called 'Danny's Diner.' "

When Bob was done, Claude was speechless, thinking, "Lord, it's awful." Bukowski didn't hold back, saying, "That's the worst song I've ever heard and the singer isn't so good either."

Bob got weepy, but he got no sympathy from Bukowski, who added, "If you play anything else I'm going to whip your ass. May I use your bathroom?"

When Bukowski was done in the bathroom they could hear him in the kitchen moving bottles around,

opening and closing doors and drawers. Bob went into his kitchen to see what was going on, and by the time Claude got there, the shouting had started.

"What the hell are you doing?"

"I'm looking for hot sauce!"

"What?!"

"You can't be a man if you don't have any hot sauce! How you going to have any punch without hot sauce, you idiot."

Bob, who couldn't believe what he was hearing, just stared at Bukowski. After a moment, he said, "Well, I think I have some somewhere." And he started looking too.

Bukowski goaded him, encouraged him to keep looking because it was so important. "Bob got his whole kitchen torn up looking for the hot sauce. Hank helped him, making a much bigger mess than necessary."

Finally, emotionally, Bob Lind conceded he might be out of hot sauce. Bukowski nodded his head, as if he'd known the truth all along. "You're just a pussy, quarter-talent. And since we don't see any woman here, and you don't have any hot sauce, you must be a queer too!"

That was it for Bob. He threw them out, screaming at Claude, "Never bring that lunatic over here again!"

Not long after this, Bukowski moved in with Linda King again, and they attempted to stay sober. Once, they visited Harold Norse, who had discovered body-building and health foods. Norse served them organic apple juice in long-stemmed wine glasses given him by Carl Weissner, who'd been over from Germany to visit. They didn't even smoke. Nevertheless, according to Norse, Bukowski managed to become argumentative and spiteful. Finally, Bukowski told Norse, "You have only one fault, baby. You've read too much Dante and Shakespeare."

Norse replied, "And your fault is you haven't read enough of them."

Occasionally, Norse would travel out to Silverlake but not to visit Bukowski and King. He was friendly with their neighbor, Anaïs Nin, who lived in a house designed by Frank Lloyd Wright, and with her companion, the great architect's stepson, Rupert Poole. There is no record of Bukowski and Nin ever meeting. Would that they had.

Linda King's home provided Bukowski a refuge from all the poets, and others, who wanted a piece of him. There were only a few of his friends who were welcome visitors, as long as they didn't abuse the privilege. Claude Powell was one of these, and he remembers the fine older homes, "sloped on easy hills overlooking this huge reservoir. Every front yard on a gentle up-hill."

Bukowski had first started going out to Silverlake so Linda could do a clay bust of him. "Hank used to laugh and gaf over how he would sit real still and drink beer at Linda's kitchen table while she worked away all serious. Then he'd start making passes and coming on to her." And such times, they usually wound up on the kitchen table along with the bust. Once their love bouts knocked the bust over and broke the nose off. "Hank used to brag that her love making matched her temper. Boy! When I heard that and thought what that must be like, it was scary."

But, now and again, a would-be poet or some other lost soul would find his way out to Silverlake. A young kid I'll call Earl Curtis made the trek. Earl for the past couple of years had been unravelling on the streets of Los Angeles. There was all that cheap dope and cheaper booze and, anyway, Charles Bukowski, the inimitable Hank, the one and only Chinaski, also called Buk, was known for living rough and if one wanted to write those great raw poems and stories, it followed that one had to live like The Man.

Earl had just lost his place at the Franklin Arms hotel downtown. He had never paid rent in that dive, indeed he didn't have a room. But he slept there

Bukowski '71
Hollywood

Claude Powell

nearly every night for eight months, sneaking into the lobby at a propitious time of evening, and scuttling behind the huge black couch directly across from the main desk.

Whether in the Franklin Arms or out on the street, Earl always had at least one yellow legal pad on his person. He would, whenever it pleased him, as Powell puts it, "take five to just drop back and write a poem right on the spot."

The kid was zealous and impressionable, his poetry mostly "unreadable." At the best of times him and it were hard to take.

So this is the young man who showed up in Silverlake one evening while Claude Powell was there. "Linda hadn't yet learned who to let in and who to keep out."

Beer appeared and after a bit of it had been consumed, Hank and Earl began to argue. Earl was the more belligerent of the two and Linda wanted him to leave. The kid refused. She threatened to call the cops. Earl began taking pokes at Hank, who endeavored to wrestle him toward the exit. As he was trying to get Earl out the door, Bukowski put his hand through one of the small glass panes. "Bleeding at the wrist, Hank went into a fit and roughed him up pretty bad."

Earl responded by putting his own fist through another pane of glass, looking at Bukowski and saying, "Isn't this the way poets act?"

Hank said "No, that ain't the way poets act! This is!"

He lifted the huge bust of himself and threw it through the large plate-glass picture window of Linda's living room. "Then he turned on Earl and told him he was next going out the window. This is how poets act!"

The only thing that saved Earl was the cops at the front door with the bust of Bukowski they had just seen come through the window. Linda ordered them to arrest both Hank and Earl.

They took the battlers to the drunk tank at L.A. County. Hank was out the next day on his own recognizance, but the kid was detained for a couple of weeks. He didn't receive proper medical attention for his cuts and by the time he was let out, his arm "was so swollen and outsized, the infection had spread into his neck and he almost got gangrene."

But the kid recovered and got a few poems out of the experience.

In October 1976, Bukowski made his very first trip out of the United States. He had been invited to Vancouver, British Columbia, to read at an arts organization called The Western Front. The gig was the brainchild of a young man named Ted Laturnus, who was knocked out by Buk's raw, aggressive style, especially, as he put it, in "view of the writers Canada tends to lionize."

Fearing Bukowski would be hassled by Customs at the Vancouver airport, Laturnus sent the writer a ticket to Seattle and arranged to pick him up. Normally a two-hour trip, there was an insane lineup at the border, so Laturnus got to spend four hours in his little MGB with his hero. "I look back on it with a combination of amusement and embarrassment."

They didn't talk much, Bukowski having told Laturnus that most people he ran into felt compelled to talk his ear off. Laturnus's main memory of Bukowski during that trip was that he seemed worried about leaving the U.S.

The Vancouver reading is described near the end of Bukowski's "novel" *Women*. For the past several years, Buk had been flying around the country, doing the readings and making up for lost time with females. He was fifty-six years old, and he'd recently met Linda Lee Beighle whom he'd marry. He was going to cut back, but not quite yet.

Laturnus felt compelled to constantly be offering the writer booze, but "he drank very little. He seemed to be pretty concerned with his health."

Bukowski was proud of his legs. Walking down the street in Vancouver, Bukowski told Laturnus, "The rest of me may be crap but I've got these great legs!"

As for the reading itself, The Western Front was packed and there was a lot of angry commotion outside from those who were barred. Laturnus was surprised to find that women in the audience far outnumbered men. He was also astounded by how nervous Bukowski was before the reading. "And he had to deal with a lot of hecklers which he did quite well."

No matter where he went during his brief Vancouver stay, Bukowski "had to fight the women off." This was a source of wonder to most guys who happened to observe Bukowski. Here, as Laturnus says, "was a man who was genuinely physically ugly," although he did have "a soothing monotone voice and a full head of hair that reminded me of Fabian."

Laturnus hosted a party afterwards, where Bukowski "was besieged with offers of congress. He eventually left with a lady who became an executive."

In his novel, Bukowski calls her Iris Hall; she has Aztec features and wasn't "obvious" like American women.

Thinking back on the experience after so many years, Laturnus's impression of Bukowski is that "he was pretty much what you read. I think he was astonished at his success and planned to milk it for all it was worth. By the time I found him, I think his hard-living days were behind him, and his main concerns were getting laid and making money so he could get laid by cleaner-smelling women."

In 1984, I started a brief correspondence with Bukowski. Over the years, I'd reviewed a few Bukowski books, and his publisher at Black Sparrow, John Martin, had shown the reviews to him. Martin suggested that I drop Bukowski a line. I hesitated doing this, having read all about people bothering him, imposing upon him. Finally, I got over my reluctance, and almost before he'd had time to receive the letter, there was an envelope in my box with drawings of airplanes all over it. And it was a great letter too, generous, funny, and opinionated.

After several days of debating with myself, I took a deep breath and mailed him some of my stories. I'd addressed and thrown away a couple of envelopes – why impose on the guy? Why should he want to read these things? How many books does he receive every week from people all over the world similarly imposing?

A few days after mailing off that book, I met a woman with whom I seemed to get along famously. I was instantly crazy about her, to tell the truth, and she seemed to like me too. We made a date for a couple of days later. A few hours before we were to meet at a restaurant downtown, I went to my post office box and there was another decorated Bukowski envelope. Much to my surprise he had kind words for my stories. Things were looking up.

After dinner and drinks that evening, we went to the woman's home and there, on the living room wall over the couch, was a large painting by Charles Bukowski. I recognized it immediately, the funny little men and women, with cigarettes and bottles of beer. He colored them in with crayons. At the bottom was Bukowski's signature and an inscription. "So" I said, "you've met Charles Bukowski?"

"Old Hank, yes."

I asked no questions. The next morning, a car appeared to take her to work. Curious, I thought, a limo at the door and a Buk on the wall.

It was a fine romance but it didn't last. We went our separate ways after a few months. In twelve years, I've only seen her briefly, across a room, passing each other on an escalator; we've exchanged only a couple of words. Until just the other day. I'd gotten a letter from Ted Laturnus recalling his experience with Bukowski, and although he didn't use her name,

Bukowski '71
Hollywood

Claude Powell

something he wrote made me think of my old friend. When I reached her on the phone, I said, "Well, I guess you're Iris Hall, aren't you?"

"Yeah, that's me or it was me."

"Was the whole thing the way he describes it?"

"Exactly."

"Did you ever see him again?"

"Sure. He sent me down to L.A. three times and we hung out. He had this court apartment in Hollywood."

"Did you know Gina and Rod and Claude?"

"Yeah. When Hank had to work, Gina and I went shopping. Claude was nice but Rod was a slime ball."

"What did you and Hank do?"

"Besides what you'd expect, we drove around a lot, went to the track, drank a bit. We never went to bars. He hated them, couldn't stand to be around one. He didn't drink any more than the rest of us. He liked good stuff, good German white wine. Mostly what we did was laugh. He was so funny. Devastatingly funny."

She said his account of their meeting was accurate. I know he got her correctly, Iris Hall, with her white skin and Aztec features.

Bukowski returned to Vancouver in 1979, to give one of his last readings. He no longer needed to do them for the money, and, having become involved with

Linda Lee Beighle, he no longer needed them for female companionship.

A guy named Dennis Del Torre had written to Bukowski, inviting him up to Vancouver to read. One afternoon, Del Torre and his friend Barrie Abbott were returning from a fishing trip, just pulling up in front of the house, when Dennis's wife came running out, saying, "Bukowski's on the phone. Really!"

Bukowski had received the invitation but wanted assurance he wasn't being kidded. "One thousand bucks and expenses." No problem, he was told.

This time Bukowski is supposed to fly directly to Vancouver, but heavy fog requires the plane to land in a town twenty-four miles away. Del Torre and Abbott pick him and Linda Lee up, and drive them to the city. It's late but Bukowski wants to go dancing. "He never wants to go dancing at home," Linda Lee says.

So they drink and dance and drink some more, and in the middle of the night, Bukowski falls out of bed in the Sylvia Hotel and has to go to the hospital for stitches. Nevertheless, he is there at dinner the next evening, surprising everyone by eating all of his health food dinner. Abbott recalls Linda Lee "goo-gooing over the host and hostess's baby and telling Buk that they should make a baby." Bukowski was "shy, quiet, reserved," and "abashed at the thought of a baby."

Linda Lee, "all blond hair and good California looks," was in a "blue dress, cut down to here." Abbott remembers thinking to himself that "poetry must be the stuff of magic, if it will bring a crater-faced, alcoholic poet, a woman such as this."

The reading was at a hall on Hasting Street, and Bukowski was drunk from the start. The crowd tried to keep up with him, and shouted, heckled. "You're not here for poetry," he told them. "You're here for blood."

They taunted him, and laughed at him, and he threatened some of them. A few wanted to read their poems, and Bukowski asked, "Do you write little poems in your mother's bathroom?"

When it just got worse, the sound system going berserk, the room getting hotter, the hollering getting louder, Bukowski wanted to know how much they'd paid to get in. "Six bucks!" someone screamed, and Bukowski replied, "I wouldn't pay six bucks to see all of you."

But the last poem, Buk got right. "Something happens to the room," says Abbott. "Just for a moment the air has a charge of what? Truth? Beauty? Life? A charge of poetry hanging in the air, like that ozone smell of lightning."

Bukowski
Hollywood '71

Claude Powell

But just as quickly as it happened, it was gone, and the great man lurches to his feet, turns his back on the audience, and "heads back to the safety of the kitchen. He's earned his thousand bucks."

Bukowski was invited to Paris to appear on the television show, *Apostrophes*, a literary interview program hosted by Bernard Pivot. There has never been anything like this show on North American television, and it is difficult for us to understand the popularity of such a thing. Over fifty million people tuned in to watch authors being asked serious questions. At least, most viewers thought the questions were serious. Bukowski, who arrived with Linda Lee on a twenty-one day excursion ticket from Los Angeles, thought the questions were inane.

He was the guest of honor, and the first to speak. Pivot asked him to in an opening statement. Bukowski, whose words were translated into French, said, "I know a great many American writers who would like to be on this program. It doesn't mean so much to me. . . ."

It just got worse. One of the other guests was a woman who wrote animal stories. Bukowski told her to show him more of her legs, and he'd be able to tell whether or not she was a good writer.

Finally, drunk, hot under the lights, and bored,

Bukowski ripped the microphone from his shirt and walked off the set.

The next morning, a critic from *Le Monde* telephoned to tell Bukowski that he had been great.

A few days after the TV "triumph," Linda Lee and Buk rode the train to Nice where her mother and uncle lived. They arrived at 11:00 p.m. after a ten-hour trip, but there was no one to meet them. Linda's uncle refused "to have a man like that in the house." They stayed in a hotel and drank, went out on the streets, but couldn't figure out the bus system. In a cafe, the waiters recognized Bukowski and applauded the great writer.

They took the train to Mannheim, Germany, where Bukowski visited his ninety-year-old Uncle Heinrich. Bukowski's uncle proved a lot friendlier than Linda's. The couple visited castles in Heidelberg, the racetrack near Düsseldorf, and the great author's birthplace at Andernach.

Upon reaching Hamburg where he was to do a reading at the Markthall, Bukowski found his name on the front pages of all the newspapers. The last reader had been Günter Grass, who drew three hundred people to the auditorium. Twelve hundred showed up for Buk, and hundreds were turned away. "The Crowd," he'd write, "was massive, animal-like, waiting."

He made his way to the stage like a heavyweight champion approaching the ring on the night of a title defence. He was nervous until he got behind his table, uncorked a bottle of white wine, and started reading. As he read, Bukowski was astonished to discover that the audience understood what he was reading. Such a thing had never happened before.

After the reading, Bukowski and Linda did more sight-seeing and returned to Paris and their plane to the United States. At L.A. Airport, they were on the escalator when Bukowski was recognized by a fan. He put down his suitcases to wave to the person, and one of them "the big Samsonite," got away, and grazed the leg of an elderly lady. She said she was okay, but her companion told her to "think it over." Bukowski was thinking "lawsuit." Finally, they got outdoors, where "a magnificent long line of yellow cabs" awaited. There was no "language barrier." It was great to be home. He never left again.

By the eighties, Bukowski had begun sending his short stories to the high-paying American glossy men's magazines. He did interviews for *Interview* and *Hustler*. He married Linda Lee Beighle in August 1983, and they moved to a suburban house in San Pedro. There Bukowski wrote ten to fifteen poems a night on his new computer. But he still sent stuff to

Bukowski
Hollywood '71

Claude Powell

what he called "the littles," the small-press places where he'd started out.

A new sort of fan began to take up Bukowski, but the man himself stayed the same. He could be drunk and obnoxious at Spago's as well as in his, her, or your, living room. Spago's is where a young writer named Gundolf Freyermuth met him in the summer of 1983. It was a Hollywood party; the insiders had their own tables at the center, while the rest were occupied by pretenders, and strays like Freyermuth and Bukowski. In *Buzz Magazine* Freyermuth describes Bukowski growing angrier as he drank, his mouth "frozen in a permanent satiated smirk." After an hour or so of this, Bukowski got to his feet and walked over to the main table where Arnold Schwarzenegger sat with his arm around his new bride Maria Shriver. "You little piece of shit!" Bukowski said to Schwarzenegger. "You and your big shitty cigar, who do you think you are? Just because you make these shitty little movies, you're nothing special, you megalomaniac piece of shit. . . ."

Arnold could only listen "helplessly, staring startled at the daring dirty old man."

He refashioned an old short story into a script for director Barbet Schroeder, and the result is the movie *Barfly*. Dennis Hopper went to see him, thinking the role of Jack Bledsoe was just for him. But Bukowski had a bad reaction to Hopper's jewelry. He liked Mickey Rourke and he liked Frank Stallone, who plays the bartender who whips him in the alley. The entire movie experience resulted in the best bit of prose Bukowski ever produced, his masterpiece, the novel *Hollywood*.

Bukowski was never a master of plot; in fact, he could not have cared less. His prose neither leaps nor sings. His prose in *Hollywood*, and everywhere else, is stripped down, bare bones. His characters neither develop nor stand in for Great Ideas. But none of this matters because Bukowski is unique. His way of looking at things elucidates all pretension and artificiality. It is so with all his writing, but in *Hollywood* he had the ideal subject matter, no better place for pretension and artificiality to be elucidated.

There is an added element to the novel *Hollywood*, something missing in his earlier work; its presence here, and in a few of his last poems, is the mark of his greatness. Yes, the word has to be applied, no matter how much it rankles. (Look, if you can't call Bukowski great, who of his contemporaries deserves it?) So the measure of the man and his achievement is that, unlike all the others, fame, instead of destroying him, turning him into that which he always hated, imbued him with a tenderness that is all the more effective, all the more powerful because it is revealed by one who has truly lived.

This is best displayed in a passage in *Hollywood* where, after house-hunting, Chinaski goes into a bar filled with bikers who recognize him, then demand he read their poems. "I paid the barkeep and we backed off our stools and moved toward the door. Again, I noticed the leather jackets and the blandness of the faces and the feeling that there wasn't much joy or daring in any of them. There was something totally missing in the poor fellows and something in me wrenched for just a moment and I felt like throwing my arms around them, consoling and embracing like some Dostoevski, but I knew that would finally lead nowhere except to ridicule and humiliation, for myself and for them. The world had somehow gone too far and spontaneous kindness could never be so easy."

That passage shows why Bukowski is a more important writer than Ernest Hemingway, to whom he has been compared more than anyone else. Hemingway, defeated by fame, believing his own manly myth, wouldn't have had the guts to write that.

Then there is the great indelible image from *Hollywood*, an image that sums up the reality of America. The filmmakers have rented a house in Venice Beach,

and after a few robberies the first week, have their doors and windows barred, locked, and chained. They sit down in the living room, thinking they're safe. While they are discussing the film about the underbelly of America, there is a noise in the wall, then a crack in the white plaster, and finally a small black hand pokes through; it rotates, fingers stretch, wriggle, hoping to grasp something to steal.

It is doubtful whether anyone cares anymore about that old bugaboo the Great American Novel. But I think it is as true as it is ironic that Charles Bukowski, in *Hollywood*, came closer than anyone ever has to writing it.

Those scores of poems he churned out at the computer in his San Pedro bedroom while drinking wine, surrounded by his cats, are hardly poems, if one thinks poems require rhyme, meter, or metaphor. In the early days, Bukowski resorted to the latter, at least. In the last days, his poems were little more than notations, lines broken willy-nilly. He drove to the racetrack in his BMW, drove to the dentist, drove to the liquor store, drove to seniors discount day at the steakhouse. He wrote about death and traffic. The only reason these are of any interest is that they are written by Bukowski, and their interest is not merely biographical. It is Bukowski talking. He doesn't look at things like anyone else. He's like Li Po on the late-twentieth-century expressway with his palm wine.

Freyermuth visited Bukowski in San Pedro a few weeks before the dirty old man died, and found him terribly diminished; his pot belly gone, clothes hanging on his bones, nearly bald after chemotherapy treatments. His movements were "executed with the slight delay of a satellite transmission, as if the commands that control his limbs come from a remote source beyond our planet." Nevertheless, he could still laugh with "malicious delight."

Bukowski's best friend in his last days was the actor Sean Penn. Bukowski's last book was a detective novel called *Pulp*. Chinaski is the private eye on Chandler's "sun-drenched streets of L.A." The case is Life, and we all know how that ends. There is a big evil bird lying in wait for the Operative, who glimpses its talons around every corner, sees the shadow of its wings beating on the sides of buildings. The bird is Death and it caught up with Bukowski on March 9, 1994. Official cause was pneumonia, which Bukowski contracted while being treated for leukemia. He was seventy-three years old, which means he cheated that bird out of a good many years.

Sean Penn's film *The Crossing Guard*, starring Jack Nicholson, was released not long after Buk died.

At the end of the film is a dedication to "my friend, Charles Bukowski. I miss you, S.P."

He's not the only one.

Bukowski is buried high above San Pedro in Green Hills Memorial Park. Below his name on the gravestone is carved the writer's philosophy of life: "Don't Try."

Bukowski's Chair
Hollywood '71

Claude Powell

"I resent death"
— Charles Bukowski